IN THE NAME OF

# ALLAH

THE ALL-COMPASSIONATE, ALL-MERCIFUL

# Problems and Solutions

- Title: Problems and Solutions
- Author: Muhammad Sâlih al-Munajjid
- English Edition 1 (1999)
- New Revised English Edition 3 (2011)
- Layout Design: IIPH, Riyadh, Saudi Arabia
- Filming and Cover Design: Samo Press Group

# Problems and Solutions

شكاوى و حلول

Muhammad Salih al-Munajjid

الدار العالمية للكتاب الإسلامي

INTERNATIONAL ISLAMIC PUBLISHING HOUSE

*King Fahd National Library Cataloging-in-Publication Data*

Al-Munajjid, Muhammad Salih
**Problems and solutions** / Muhammad Salih al-Munajjid .- Riyadh, 2011

64 p ; 21 cm

ISBN Paperback: 978-603-501-101-3

1- Problem solving 2- Reasoning 3- Thought and thinking
I- Title

153.43 dc 1432/4112

Legal Deposit no. **1432/4112**
ISBN Paperback: **978-603-501-101-3**



International Islamic Publishing House (IIPH)
P.O. Box 55195 Riyadh 11534, Saudi Arabia
Tel: 966 1 4650818 / 4647213 — Fax: 966 1 4633489
E-mail: iiph@iiph.com.sa — iiphsa@gmail.com
www.iiph.com.sa

# Contents

## Pronunciation and Transliteration Chart

| Arabic script | Pronunciation | Transliterated as: |
|---|---|---|
| أ | short 'a', as in *cat* | a |
| آ - ى | longer 'a', as in *cab* (not as in *cake*) | â |
| ب | /b/ as in *bell*, *rubber* and *tab* | b |
| ت | /t/ as in *tap, mustard* and *sit* | t |
| ة | takes the sound of the preceding diactrical mark sometimes ending in h (when in pausal form): ah, ih, or ooh; or atu(n), ati(n) or ata(n) when in uninterrupted speech | h or t (when followed by another Arabic word) |
| ث | /th/ as in *thing*, *maths* and *wealth* | th |
| ج | /j/ as in *jam*, *ajar* and *age* | j |
| ح | a 'harsher' sound than the English initial /h/, and may occur medially and in word-final position as well | ḥ |
| خ | as in *Bach* (in German); may occur initially and medially as well | kh |
| د | /d/ as in *do*, *muddy* and *red* | d |
| ذ | as in *this*, *father*, and *with* | dh |
| ر | /r/ as in *raw*, *art* and *war*; may also be a rolled r, as with Spanish words | r |

| Arabic script | Pronunciation | Transliterated as: |
|---|---|---|
| ز | /z/ as in *zoo*, *easy* and *gaze* | z |
| س | /s/ as in *so*, *messy* and *grass* | s |
| ش | as in *ship*, *ashes* and *rush* | sh |
| ص | no close equivalent in English, but may be approximated by pronouncing it as /sw/ or /s/ farther back in the mouth | ṣ |
| ض | no close equivalent in English, but may be approximated by pronouncing /d/ farther back in the mouth | ḍ |
| ط | no close equivalent in English, but may be approximated by pronouncing /t/ farther back in the mouth | ṭ |
| ظ | no close equivalent in English, but may be approximated by pronouncing 'the' farther back in the mouth | <u>dh</u> |
| ع | no close equivalent in English: a guttural sound in the back of the throat | ʿ |
| غ | no close equivalent in English, but may be closely approximated by pronouncing it like the French /r/ in 'rouge' | gh |
| ف | /f/ as in *fill*, *effort* and *muff* | f |

| Arabic script | Pronunciation | Transliterated as: |
|---|---|---|
| ق | no close equivalent in English, but may be approximated by pronouncing /k/ farther back in the mouth | q |
| ك | /k/ as in *king*, *buckle* and *tack* | k |
| ل | /l/ as in *lap*, *halo*; in the word *Allah*, it becomes velarized as in *ball* | l |
| م | /m/ as in *men*, *simple* and *ram* | m |
| ن | /n/ as in *net*, *ant* and *can* | n |
| هـ – ه – ـه | /h/ as in hat; unlike /h/ in English, in Arabic /h/ is pronounced in medial and word-final positions as well | h |
| و | as in *wet* and *away* | w |
| و (as a vowel) | long u, as in *boot* and *too* | oo |
| ي | as in *yet* and *yard* | y |
| ي (as a vowel) | long e, as in *eat*, *beef* and *see* | ee |
| ء | glottal stop: may be closely approximated by pronouncing it like ‘t’ in the Cockney English pronunciation of *butter*: *bu’er*, or the stop sound in *uh — oh!* | ’ (Omitted in initial position) |

**Diphthongs:**

| **Arabic script** | **Pronunciation** | **Transliterated as:** |
|---|---|---|
| أوَ ، و | Long o, as in *owe*, *boat* and *go* | au, aw, ow |
| أي ، يَ | Long ‘a’, as in *able*, *rain* and *say* | ay, ai, ei |

**Diacritical marks (*tashkeel*):**

| **Name of mark** | **Pronunciation** | **Transliterated as:** |
|---|---|---|
| ـَ<br>fatḥah | very short ‘a’ or schwa (unstressed vowel) | a |
| ـِ<br>kasrah | shorter version of ee or schwa (unstressed vowel) | i |
| ـُ<br>Dammah | shorter version of oo | u |
| ـّ<br>shaddah | a doubled consonant is stressed in the word, and the length of the sound is also doubled | Double letter |
| ـْ<br>sukoon | no vowel sound between consonants or at the end of a word | Absence of vowel |

# Arabic honorific symbols used in this book

(سبحانه وتعالى): *Subḥânahu wa ta'âlâ* — 'The Exalted'

(صلى الله عليه وسلم): *Ṣalla-Allâhu 'alayhi wa sallam* — 'Blessings and peace be upon him'

(عليه السلام): *'Alayhis-salâm* — 'Peace be upon him'

(رضي الله عنه): *Raḍiya Allâhu 'anhu* — 'May Allah be pleased with <u>him</u>'

(رضي الله عنها): *Raḍiya Allâhu 'anhâ* — 'May Allah be pleased with <u>her</u>'

## About the word 'Lord'

The word *lord* in English has several related meanings. The original meaning is 'master' or 'ruler', and in this sense it is often used to refer to human beings: 'the lord of the mansion' or 'Lord So-and-So' (in the United Kingdom, for example). The word *Lord* with a capital L is used in the lexicon of Islam to refer to the One and Only God — Allah. In Islam, there is no ambiguity about the meaning of this word. While it is true that one may occasionally use the word *lord* (whether capitalized or not) to refer to a human being, in Islamic discourse the reference of this term is always clear from the context. Whereas for Christians, Hindus and other polytheists, the word *Lord* with a capital 'L' may refer to Allah, to Jesus or to some imagined deity, for Muslims, there can be no plurality of meaning. Allah alone is the Lord, and the Lord is Allah — not Jesus, not Rama, not any other being.

The Editor

## When 'jihad' refers to fighting

Although jihad is often translated into English as 'holy war', it must be noted that war has never been described as 'holy' in any of Islam's primary texts or even early Islamic literature. Linguistically speaking, jihad is an Islamic term that applies to a broad spectrum of activities, ranging from daily striving to meet the day's challenges, to the striving against one's desires and self, to the struggle to provide for one's family. Its basic definition is 'the act of striving or struggling in the way of Allah'. Therefore, jihad is not limited to war; it includes struggling with one's soul, speech, body and wealth so that the message of Allah reaches all humans willing to receive it.

Islamic scholars have referred to different types of jihad, such as jihad against the self (to understand Islam, act upon it, call others to it and be patient with the difficulties of making this call), jihad against the Devil (repelling Satanic whispers, doubts and lusts), jihad against the tongue (controlling it, using it to enjoin what is good, forbid what is wrong, spread the correct teachings of Islam and answer false ideologies), jihad against aggression (with the purpose of protecting Islam and the lives, honour and property of Muslims) and other types of jihad like jihad against the hypocrites, jihad against oppressors and jihad against mischief makers.

Jihad — in the context of fighting — has specific rules and conditions that need to be met before jihad is initiated. The first rule is that people are not to be fought because of what they believe, or to coerce them to accept Islam. The second rule is to 'fight only those who fight you' and never initiate unprovoked aggression *(Qur'an 2: 190)*. That means that Muslims are only allowed to fight back, rather than initiating fighting; but 'fighting back' includes fighting against actual aggression as well as proactively addressing real threats of aggression. In both cases, Muslims are instructed to be prepared and ready to defend their nation before they actually engage in military conflict. There are additional conditions, but the above-mentioned conditions are vital for putting jihad in its broader meaning in the proper context.

Another condition of the sort of jihad which involves fighting is that it should take place only under an Islamic authority that 'raises the banner' for such jihad. It is not following the Sunnah at all for any individual or self-appointed group of Muslims to wage war on behalf of a nation. Instead, Muslims should be united under the single authority of an imam or khaleefah (caliph), except in the case where an individual needs to defend his own family and property, or to help his neighbour to do so. This is proved by the example of the early Muslims as well as texts in the Qur'an and the Sunnah:

﴾When there comes to them [the hypocrites] a matter related to [public] safety or fear, they spread it about; if only they had referred it to the Messenger and to such of them as are in authority, those among them who are able to think through the matter would have understood it.﴿ *(Qur'an 4: 83)*

«Ḥudhayfah ibn Yaman asked the Prophet (ﷺ): What if (the Muslims) have no single leader (they are divided into disputing groups)? The Prophet (ﷺ) answered: If they have no single leader or unified group, then leave all these disputing groups, even if you have to bite on a tree until your death.» (part of a longer hadith recorded by Bukhari)

There are other conditions for jihad. In general, the rules laid out for war in Islam should be upheld unless there is some legitimate need or strategy when fighting occurs that would necessitate going against those rules. A Muslim should not kill himself or herself *(Qur'an 4: 29)* nor kill another Muslim, except by accident *(Qur'an 4: 92)*. Women, children, the elderly and other non-combatants should not be harmed. Land should not be destroyed, nor trees cut down. Corpses should not be mutilated. Islam should not be imposed upon non-believers. Rather, if combatant non-Muslims choose on their own to embrace Islam, even if only as a deceitful trick, it should be accepted by the Muslim leadership, and fighting should stop. Peace should be sought before lives are lost. Treaties and agreements should be upheld. Prisoners should be well-treated. Above all, justice must be done.

﴾Fight in the path [according to the rules set by Allah] of Allah only those who fight you, but do not commit aggression [transgress limits]. Allah does not love aggressors. ...And fight them until persecution is no more, and religion is [freely embraced] for [the individual's faith in] Allah. But if they desist, then let there be no aggression except against transgressors.﴿

*(Qur'an 2: 190, 193)*

﴾Allah does not forbid you from being good, kind, just, and fair to those who have not fought you because of religion nor driven you from your homeland. Allah loves those who are just. Allah forbids you from giving allegiance to those who have fought you because of religion and have driven you from your homeland, and those who supported your expulsion...﴿ *(Qur'an 60: 8-9)*

In addition, the Muslim nation is encouraged to maintain strong military capabilities to promote justice and to deter acts of war and aggression.

﴾And make ready for them [their potential aggression] all you can of power, including steeds of war, to deter the enemy of Allah and your enemy, and others besides, whom you may not know but whom Allah knows.﴿ *(Qur'an 8: 60)*

The Editor

## Publisher's Note

All praise and thanks belong to Allah alone, the One, the Almighty and All-Merciful. Blessings and peace be upon Prophet Muhammad, the last of His messengers and prophets, and upon his family, his Companions, and all those who follow in their footsteps until the end of time.

There are various problems which a Muslim faces at an individual level. Some of these include an ill temper and excessive laughter. Such issues may seem trivial, however, if they are not addressed immediately, they can become very problematic for those who are genuinely striving to practice their religion, and can affect those around the affected individual as well.

In this book, the author has addressed a few issues a Muslim might face from time to time. He has presented a theoretical as well as practical analysis of each issue and offered a range of solutions. It is hoped that the readers will find this information useful and apply some of the techniques in their daily lives to resolve their individual problems.

May Allah accept the efforts of all those who contributed to the production of this book, and may it be acceptable to Him, *âmeen*.

Muhammad Abdul Mohsin Al-Tuwaijri

Managing Director
International Islamic Publishing House
Riyadh, Saudi Arabia

# Introduction

All praise is for Allah (*Subḥânahu wa Ta'âlâ* — Glorified and Exalted is He). We praise Him and seek His help; we also seek refuge with Allah (ﷻ) from the evil of our own selves and from our evil deeds. No one can misguide the one whom Allah (ﷻ) leads to the straight path. Similarly, no one can guide the one whom He allows to go astray. I bear witness that there is no true god except Allah (ﷻ) alone, with no partner or associate. I also bear witness that Muhammad (*ṣalla Allâhu 'alayhi wa sallam* — blessings and peace be upon him) is His slave and messenger.

﴿يَٰٓأَيُّهَا ٱلَّذِينَ ءَامَنُوا۟ ٱتَّقُوا۟ ٱللَّهَ حَقَّ تُقَاتِهِۦ وَلَا تَمُوتُنَّ إِلَّا وَأَنتُم مُّسْلِمُونَ ﴿١٠٢﴾﴾

(سورة آل عِمرَان: ١٠٢)

﴾O you who have believed, fear Allah as He should be feared and do not die except as Muslims [in submission to Him].﴿

*(Qur'an 3: 102)*[1]

﴿يَٰٓأَيُّهَا ٱلنَّاسُ ٱتَّقُوا۟ رَبَّكُمُ ٱلَّذِى خَلَقَكُم مِّن نَّفْسٍ وَٰحِدَةٍ وَخَلَقَ مِنْهَا زَوْجَهَا وَبَثَّ مِنْهُمَا رِجَالًا كَثِيرًا وَنِسَآءً ۚ وَٱتَّقُوا۟ ٱللَّهَ ٱلَّذِى تَسَآءَلُونَ بِهِۦ وَٱلْأَرْحَامَ ۚ إِنَّ ٱللَّهَ كَانَ عَلَيْكُمْ رَقِيبًا ﴿١﴾﴾

(سورة النِّسَاء: ١)

---

[1] The translations of the meanings of the Qur'anic verses in this book have been adapted from: Ṣaḥeeḥ International. *The Qur'an: Arabic Text with Corresponding English Meaning*. Jeddah: Abul Qâsim Publishing House, 1997

﴾O humankind, fear your Lord, who created you from one soul and created from it its mate and dispersed from both of them many men and women. And fear Allah, through whom you ask one another, and the wombs [in regard to relations of kinship]. Indeed Allah is ever, over you, an Observer.﴿ *(Qur'an 4: 1)*

﴿يَٰٓأَيُّهَا ٱلَّذِينَ ءَامَنُواْ ٱتَّقُواْ ٱللَّهَ وَقُولُواْ قَوۡلٗا سَدِيدٗا ٧٠ يُصۡلِحۡ لَكُمۡ أَعۡمَٰلَكُمۡ
وَيَغۡفِرۡ لَكُمۡ ذُنُوبَكُمۡۗ وَمَن يُطِعِ ٱللَّهَ وَرَسُولَهُۥ فَقَدۡ فَازَ فَوۡزًا عَظِيمًا ٧١﴾

(سورة الأحزاب: ٧٠-٧١)

﴾O you who have believed, fear Allah and speak words of appropriate justice. He will [then] amend for you your deeds and forgive you your sins. And whoever obeys Allah and His Messenger has certainly attained a great attainment.﴿

*(Qur'an 33: 70-71)*

Some people ask me questions in various talks and lectures I deliver, including questions about a number of problems regarding 'diseases of the heart' (spiritual problems) and very real obstacles they are facing. I have answered some of these in a series of studies entitled *Shakâwa wa Ḥulool* (*Problems and Solutions*).

This series has been reviewed for publication, and I now present it to my brothers and sisters in the hope that this may help me to be among those referred to in the following *hadith* [a statement of the Prophet Muhammad (ﷺ) that was remembered and recorded by his Companions and followers]: «Whoever relieves a believer of some of the distress of this world, Allah will relieve him of some of the distress on the Day of Judgement... Allah will help His slave as long as the slave helps his brother.» (Muslim)

I ask Allah the Almighty to give my brothers and sisters, and myself, the strength to do good deeds and avoid evil, and to save us on the day of regrets; indeed, He is the Best of those who are asked and He is Able to do all things.

Shaykh Muhammad Ṣaliḥ al-Munajjid

بِسْمِ ٱللَّهِ ٱلرَّحْمَٰنِ ٱلرَّحِيمِ

*In the name of Allah, the All-Compassionate, All-Merciful*

# Missing *ṣalât al-fajr* (the dawn prayer)

A brother complained: "I miss ṣalât al-fajr on most days; I hardly ever pray it at the right time. Usually, I do not wake up until after the sun has risen. At best, I wake up after having missed the congregation for fajr prayers. I have tried to wake up at the right time with no success. What is the solution to this problem?"

All praise is for Allah (ﷻ). The solution to this problem, like others, has two aspects: theoretical and practical.

## Theoretical solution

The theoretical aspect can be further broken down into two points:

1. Muslims should know the great status of ṣalât al-fajr in the sight of Allah (ﷻ), as explained in the following hadiths.

«Whoever prays the dawn prayer in congregation, it is as if he had prayed for the whole night.» (Muslim and at-Tirmidhi)

«The most burdensome prayers for the hypocrites are *ṣalât al-'ishâ'* (the obligatory night prayer) and ṣalât al-fajr; if they only knew what they contain, they would come even if they had to crawl.» (Aḥmad; al-Albâni graded it as sound)

«Whoever prays fajr [on time] is under the protection of Allah...» (Muslim)

«Angels come to you in shifts by night and by day. They meet at ṣalât al-fajr and *ṣalât al-'aṣr* (the afternoon prayer); those who had stayed with you at night ascend and are asked by the One Who knows better than they: How did you find My slaves? They say: We left them when they were praying, and we came to them when they were praying.» (Bukhari)

«The best of prayers in the sight of Allah is the dawn prayer on Friday, in congregation.» (Abu Na'eem; al-Albâni graded it as sound)

«Whoever prays the fajr and 'aṣr prayers will enter paradise.» (Bukhari)

2. Muslims should understand the seriousness of missing ṣalât al-fajr. This is explained by the aforementioned hadith: «The most burdensome prayers for the hypocrites are ṣalât al-'ishâ' and ṣalât al-fajr...»

Ibn 'Umar (*raḍiya Allâhu 'anhu* — may Allah be pleased with him) said: If we did not see a person at fajr and 'ishâ' prayers, we would think badly of him. (Recorded by aṭ-Ṭabarâni with a trustworthy chain of narrators)

They thought badly of a person who was absent from these two prayers because their regular performance is an indication of people's faith and a measure of their sincerity. Other prayers may be easier to perform because they are more convenient to their circumstances and fit in with their work and sleep routines. However, only the determined and sincere believers, whom one hopes are good, will be able to pray fajr and 'ishâ' regularly (in congregation, for men).

Another hadith, part of which was quoted previously, indicates the seriousness of missing ṣalât al-fajr: «Whoever prays fajr [on time] is under the protection of Allah. Do not put yourselves in a situation where Allah has to call you to account for your negligence, because whoever finds himself in this situation will be sorted out and then thrown on his face in the fire of hell.» (Muslim)

These two points are sufficient to guarantee that the hearts of Muslims will be concerned about not missing fajr. Firstly, they should be motivated to strive and earn the reward for fajr; secondly, they should pay heed to the aforementioned hadith's warning and avoid the sin of negligence.

## Practical solution

The practical aspect of dealing with this problem includes a number of steps which Muslims can take in order to become more accustomed to performing ṣalât al-fajr regularly and in congregation. These steps include:

1. Sleeping early: The Prophet (ﷺ) used to dislike sleeping before 'ishâ' and talking afterwards. (mentioned by 'Abdur-Razzâq in his Muṣannaf; al-Albâni graded it as sound)

Muslims should not sleep before ṣalât al-'ishâ' because it is obvious that most of those who sleep before it will spend the rest of the night feeling as tired and heavy as if they were ill.

Muslims should not linger and talk after 'ishâ'; the scholars have explained the reason why doing so is disliked. They explain that talking after 'ishâ' leads to people staying up late, which in turns leads to the fear that they will sleep and miss *qiyâm al-layl* (the optional night prayer) or the correct or preferred time for fajr prayer.

The kind of talk that is disliked after 'ishâ', as the commentators explain, is that in which there is no clear benefit. However, if there is some benefit — such as studying and gaining knowledge, learning stories of righteous people, speaking to a guest, spending time with one's wife and family, speaking to travellers and taking care of them and their luggage, or any other permissible reason — then there is nothing wrong with it. This has no connection with the reasons for which many people stay up late nowadays: to do wrong and commit sins! Muslims should sleep early so that they can wake up refreshed to pray fajr; they should avoid late nights that make them too tired to get up and pray fajr (in congregation, for men).

It is a fact that people differ with regard to their need for sleep. It is not possible to dictate a set number of hours that everyone should sleep; rather, individuals should stick to the time that will give them enough sleep to wake up refreshed for ṣalât al-fajr. If a man knows from experience that sleeping after 11 p.m., for example, will mean that he cannot get up for fajr, then from an Islamic point of view, he should not sleep any later than that.

2. Ensuring that they are in state of ritual purity, and reciting prayers and invocations before sleeping: this helps people to get up for fajr.

3. Having a sincere intention and being determined, when going to sleep, to get up for fajr. Those who go to sleep hoping that the alarm will not go off and that no one will come and wake them up, will not be able to get up to pray fajr as long as they harbour this bad intention.

4. Remembering Allah (سبحانه وتعالى) immediately upon waking up: Some

people habitually wake up and then go back to sleep. However, if they remember Allah (ﷻ) straight after waking up, this will loosen one of the knots of the devil and motivate them to get up. When they perform ablution, their determination will become stronger, and Satan will be driven further away; when they pray, their devil will be defeated, their balance [of good deeds] will become heavier and they will feel happy and energetic. (Bukhari)

5. Seeking help from family and friends to pray fajr on time and encouraging one another in this regard: This is essential and is undoubtedly included in the following words of Allah (ﷻ):

﴿... وَتَعَاوَنُوا عَلَى الْبِرِّ وَالتَّقْوَىٰ ... ﴿٢﴾﴾ (سورة المائدة: ٢)

﴿...And cooperate in righteousness and piety...﴾ *(Qur'an 5: 2)*

﴿وَالْعَصْرِ ﴿١﴾ إِنَّ الْإِنسَانَ لَفِي خُسْرٍ ﴿٢﴾ إِلَّا الَّذِينَ آمَنُوا وَعَمِلُوا الصَّالِحَاتِ
وَتَوَاصَوْا بِالْحَقِّ وَتَوَاصَوْا بِالصَّبْرِ ﴿٣﴾﴾ (سورة العصر: ١-٣)

﴿By time. Indeed, humankind is in loss, except for those who have believed and done righteous deeds and advised each other to truth and advised each other to patience.﴾ *(Qur'an 103: 1-3)*

A Muslim man should encourage his wife by waking her up to pray fajr, and she should encourage him, no matter how tired and exhausted they may be. Children should also seek their parents' help to wake up when it is time for prayer. No parent should say: "They have exams; they are tired. Let them sleep, poor kids." It is a mistake to believe that by doing this, one is being a kind and merciful parent; true parental mercy means waking them up to worship Allah (ﷻ).

﴿وَأْمُرْ أَهْلَكَ بِالصَّلَاةِ وَاصْطَبِرْ عَلَيْهَا ... ﴿١٣٢﴾﴾ (سورة طه: ١٣٢)

﴾And enjoin prayer upon your family [and people] and be steadfast therein...﴿ *(Qur'an 20: 132)*

Just as family members should help and encourage one another to pray fajr, so too should brothers and sisters in Islam. For example, university students living in the same residence, or neighbours in the same neighbourhood, can help one another by knocking on a neighbour's door to wake them up for prayer and encourage them to worship Allah (ﷻ).

6. Praying to Allah (ﷻ) to help them wake up for fajr (in congregation, for men). Supplication is one of the greatest sources of strength and success in all things.

7. Using various means of being woken up, such as alarm clocks. These should be put in the most appropriate place. Some people put the alarm clock next to their head; when it rings, they turn it off at once and go straight back to sleep. Instead, they should put the clock a little further away, so that it proves more effective in really waking them up.

They can also arrange to receive alarm calls from the telephone company; Muslims should not think that it is too much to pay for this service if they really need it, because this will be considered as spending in the way of Allah (ﷻ). Also, waking up to obey the command of Allah (ﷻ) cannot be measured in terms of worldly wealth. They can also seek the help of brothers, sisters or friends to wake them up in a similar manner.

8. Sprinkling water on the face of the sleeping person: «The Prophet (ﷺ) praised the man who gets up at night to pray and wakes up his wife; when she refuses to get up, he sprinkles water on her face. He also praised the woman who gets up at night to pray and wakes up her husband; when he refuses to get up, she

sprinkles water on his face.» (Aḥmad; al-Albâni graded it as sound)

Sprinkling water on a sleeping person's face is one of the means prescribed by the Sharia for waking someone for prayer. In fact, it is quite refreshing and energising. Some people may become enraged when awakened in this manner; they may shout, swear and issue threats. Therefore, the person who is seeking to wake another should employ wisdom and patience and should also remember that the pens are lifted from the record of the one who is sleeping (that is, their deeds are not being recorded while they are asleep). Therefore, one should patiently bear negative responses and not be discouraged from trying to wake people for prayer.

9. Refraining from sleeping alone: «The Prophet (ﷺ) forbade any man to sleep alone.» (Aḥmad; al-Albâni graded it as sound)

Perhaps the wisdom behind this prohibition is that people could sleep too long if there is no one to wake them up for prayer.

10. Refraining from sleeping in remote places where it would not occur to anyone that someone might be sleeping, without informing anyone — such as the roof of a house or a remote part of a house or student residence. In this case, no one will know that they need to be awakened for prayer; instead, everyone might even think that they are in the mosque when, in fact, they are fast asleep. Anyone who needs to sleep in a remote place should tell people where they will be, so that the others can come and wake them up.

11. Being lively and active upon waking: They should get up at once and not awaken in stages, as some people do. These people might be awoken several times, getting up each time, but once

their friend has left, they go back to bed. Waking up in stages usually ends in failure; the only way to prevent falling asleep again is to get up right away.

12. Not setting the alarm too early: If people know that there is still a long time to go before the time for prayer ends, they may think, "I still have time, let me sleep a little more..." They should set the alarm at an appropriate time to avoid this situation.

13. Lighting a lamp upon waking up — or, in our modern times, turning on the light: This has the effect of dispelling sleepiness.

14. Not staying up late, even to pray qiyâm al-layl: Some people stay up late to pray qiyâm al-layl and then fall asleep a few minutes before fajr and are unable to wake up for the prayer. This happens a lot in Ramadan — people stay up late and fall asleep just before fajr, so they end up missing the prayer entirely. This is undoubtedly a grave error, because obligatory prayer should take precedence over supererogatory prayer. So what about those who stay up late not to pray but to commit sin, or at best, to do permissible things? Satan may make the idea of staying up late to discuss important matters attractive to some callers to Islam; they might then sleep late and miss the prayer, thus losing much more than they gained.

15. Not eating too much before going to sleep: Eating too much causes deep sleep. Those who eat a lot get very tired and sleep a lot, thus losing a lot. They should try to eat lightly in the evening.

16. Warning about the misinterpretation of the Sunnah to lie down after praying the sunnah prayer before fajr: Some people may have heard the hadith in which the Prophet (ﷺ) said: «When any one of you has prayed, let him lie down on his right side.» (at-Tirmidhi; al-Albâni graded it as sound)

It is also reported that after the Prophet (ﷺ) prayed the sunnah of fajr, he would lie down. Then Bilâl (رضي الله عنه) would call him to prayer, and he would stand up to pray. People may have heard these hadiths and be keen to follow this proven Sunnah, but they do not understand how to do it properly. They might pray the sunnah of fajr, lie down on their right side, and fall fast asleep until the sun rises. This is because of a lack of proper understanding. The lying down is not for the purpose of sleeping. Bilâl (رضي الله عنه) used to come and tell the Prophet (ﷺ) when it was time to pray. Moreover, as is reported by Imam Aḥmad and Ibn Ḥibbân in an authentic hadith: «If the Prophet (ﷺ) wanted to rest before fajr, he would put his head on his right palm, propped up on his elbow.» (Aḥmad; al-Albâni graded it as sound)

This kind of resting prevents one from falling fast asleep; since the head is propped up by the palm and elbow, it will drop if the person dozes off, and he or she will wake up again. In addition to this, Bilâl (رضي الله عنه) was entrusted with the responsibility of waking the Prophet (ﷺ) for the fajr prayer if he did fall asleep.

17. Praying qiyâm al-layl late at night, just before fajr, so that soon after they finish *witr* (a single unit of prayer prayed at night), the call for fajr prayer is given, making the worship continuous. The night prayer should be offered during the last third of the night — which is the preferred time — and immediately followed by the fajr prayer, while one is awake and energetic.

18. Following the example of the Prophet (ﷺ) when lying down to sleep: A person should lie on the right side, placing the right cheek on the right hand. This position makes it easy to wake up. The best guidance is the guidance of Muhammad (ﷺ), and this is better than sleeping in any other position which may make it difficult to wake up for fajr prayer.

19. Helping themselves by taking a nap during the day because this will help them need less sleep at night.

20. Not sleeping after ṣalât al-'aṣr or *ṣalât al-maghrib* (the sunset prayer): this will make people go to bed late, and whoever goes to bed late will find it difficult to wake up early.

21. Finally, sincere devotion to Allah (ﷻ) is the best thing to motivate people to get up for prayer; this is because Allah is the One Who is controlling all means of help. If believers have that true sincerity, and their hearts are full of devotion to Allah (ﷻ), Allah (ﷻ) will help them get up and pray fajr (in congregation, for men) even if they doze off only a few moments before fajr.

This sincerity and devotion may cause some very enthusiastic people to find unusual ways to help themselves to wake up to pray, which is a sign of their eagerness and keenness. Some of them may set a number of alarm clocks to wake them up, setting each one a few minutes later than the other; thus, even if they turn the first one off, the next one will wake them a few moments later, and so on. Another may tie a string to his wrist, with the other end dangling from his window, so that when one of his friends passes by on his way to the mosque, he can pull on the string, hence, waking him for fajr prayer.

A lot can be achieved with sincerity and determination; may Allah (ﷻ) guide us! However, the bitter truth is that weakness of faith and lack of sincerity are widespread among people nowadays, as we can see from the small numbers of people found in the mosques praying fajr in congregation. This is despite the fact that there are many people living around the mosques in many neighbourhoods.

However, without doubt, there are people who sleep so heavily that it is almost like an illness; they may be excused because the matter is beyond their control. People in this situation should turn to Allah (ﷻ) for help, visit a doctor, and do everything that they possibly can to try to find a cure.

Finally, a word about a well-known phenomenon: some people claim that there is a hadith which says that those who want to get up for fajr should recite the last part of *Soorat* (chapter of the Qur'an) *al-Kahf* before sleeping, firmly intending to get up at a certain hour, and that will enable them to get up at that time. They claim that this is a tried and tested method. Our response is that there is no such authentic hadith. Therefore, this carries no weight as evidence whatsoever, and ultimately, the best guidance is the guidance of Muhammad (ﷺ).

## Excessive laughter

This is a widespread problem, especially among the youth. Someone asked: "Our gatherings with friends and colleagues are filled with too much laughter; it goes to extremes. This phenomenon is becoming ever more widespread. What is the solution?"

### Theoretical solution

The theoretical aspect may be further broken down into two points:

Firstly, we should know how the Prophet (ﷺ) always conducted himself when it came to laughter; he is the best example in this case, as in all other things.

It is reported in one hadith that: «His [the Prophet's] laughter was never more than a smile.» (Aḥmad; al-Albâni graded it as sound)

According to another hadith: «The Prophet (ﷺ) used to remain silent for long periods and laugh little.» (Aḥmad; al-Albâni graded it as sound)

'Â'ishah (*raḍiya Allâhu 'anhâ* — may Allah be pleased with her) narrated: «I never saw the Messenger of Allah laughing so heartily that his back teeth were visible; he would only smile.» (Bukhari)

According to an authentic hadith, the Prophet (ﷺ) said: «Do not laugh too much, for excessive laughter kills the heart [spiritually].» (Ibn Mâjah; al-Albâni graded it as sound)

According to another report, he said: «... too much laughter corrupts the heart.» (Ibn Mâjah and at-Tirmidhi; al-Albâni graded it as sound)

After knowing all this, if Muslims laugh excessively, it is akin to undertaking a journey that they know will lead to punishment. This is the theoretical response to this problem, in brief.

Before we turn to the practical aspects, we must point out that laughter is not unlawful in Sharia; Muslims are not expected to be stern and rigid at all times. Laughter is quite natural, and indeed Allah (ﷻ) says in the Qur'an:

﴿وَأَنَّهُۥ هُوَ أَضْحَكَ وَأَبْكَىٰ ﴿٤٣﴾﴾ (سورة النّجْم: ٤٣)

﴿And that it is He who makes [one] laugh and weep.﴾

*(Qur'an 53: 43)*

However, the problem which we are discussing here — excessive laughter — has a number of negative effects, including the following:

1. It makes gatherings explode with echoing, unpleasant laughter.
2. The hearts of the believers are spiritually corrupted by too much laughter; they open their mouths too wide, instead of being serious and portraying a sound character.
3. Some callers to Islam make people laugh as a means of winning them over and influencing them, or so they claim. What they do not realise is that people gather around them only for the sake of laughter and therefore do not benefit from them at all.

The problem is that some people use laughter as a safety valve, in order to release their stress and worries. Hence, they resort to an inferior means rather than the superior ones.

I remember a young man who was suffering from anxiety because he was behind in his studies; he was going through some family problems and other troubles as well. One day he went out of his house and ran into a friend, who asked him: "Where are you going?" He replied: "I am worried and stressed out, so I'm going to see so-and-so; he can make me laugh and forget my problems..." He did not realize that his friend's ability to make him laugh was like a drug; it makes people forget their troubles while they are under its influence, but when it wears off, everything remains as it was before.

Muslims should know better. They should treat worries and stress in the way prescribed by the Prophet (ﷺ): «When something was troubling him, he would pray.» (a sound hadith recorded by Abu Dâwood)

«If something distressed him, he would say: *Yâ Ḥayyu yâ Qayyoom, bi raḥmatika astagheethu* (O Ever-Living, O Eternal

One, by Your mercy I seek Your help).» (at-Tirmidhi; a similar hadith has been graded sound by al-Albâni)

According to another authentic hadith, when he was overtaken by worries and distress, he would say: «*Yâ Ḥayyu yâ Qayyoom, bi raḥmatika astagheethu. Allâhu rabbi wa lâ ushriku bihi shay'an* (O Ever-Living, O Eternal One, by Your mercy I seek Your help. Allah is my Lord, and I do not associate anything with Him).» (Abu Dâwood; al-Albâni graded it as sound)

In the famous supplication to relieve stress and anxiety, he said: «*Allâhumma inni 'abduka, wa'bnu 'abdika wa'bnu amatika...* (O Allah, I am Your slave, the son of Your slave and the son of Your maidservant...)» (recorded in Ṣawâ'iq al-Mursalah; Ibn Qayyim graded it as sound)

## Practical solutions

Now that this concept has been understood properly, we move on to the discussion of the practical ways of dealing with the problem of excessive laughter. This problem can be dealt with in the following ways:

1. Remembering death, the grave, the day of reckoning, the bridge over paradise that passes over hell, the hellfire and all the other terrors of the hereafter. The way to remember all these things is to read the texts that describe these scenes and to study their details and commentaries; it would also be useful to sit with ascetic people and those whose hearts are devoted to Allah (ﷻ).

2. Thinking about the situation of the Muslims and how they are suffering because they have strayed from their religion; they are behind in all the fields of life, facing oppression, hardship and

destruction; they are also subject to the plots of international conspiracies. Muslims think long and hard about this situation, it has an impact on how much they laugh and cry.

3. Feeling the weight of their great responsibility towards their *Ummah* (the community of believers in Islam), which requires huge efforts to save it from the danger of falling. If this becomes their concern, they will start making active efforts to reform their family, friends and society as much as they can. They will not have time for telling silly jokes, laughing excessively or engaging in trivial pursuits.

4. Avoiding mixing with jokers who are well-known for making people laugh and trying to be funny, and trying to stay away from the gatherings in which they are present, while also trying to advise them and the people who sit with them to be serious. We have already referred to some callers to Islam who use the tactic of making people laugh as a means of winning people's attention. In some cases, the general public may say: "Where is the shaykh who makes us laugh? We want the shaykh who makes us laugh!" This is a step backwards, which we hope the Ummah will avoid, because the religion of Allah is great and strong. Allah (ﷻ) says:

﴿إِنَّهُۥ لَقَوْلٌ فَصْلٌ ۝١٣ وَمَا هُوَ بِٱلْهَزْلِ ۝١٤﴾ (سورة الطّارق: ١٣-١٤)

﴾Indeed, it [the Qur'an] is a decisive statement, and it is not amusement.﴿ *(Qur'an 86: 13-14)*

And:

﴿... خُذُواْ مَآ ءَاتَيْنَٰكُم بِقُوَّةٍ ... ۝٩٣﴾ (سورة البَقَرَة: ٩٣)

﴾...Take what We have given you with determination...﴿ *(Qur'an 2: 93)*

The Prophet (ﷺ) said: «If you knew what I know, you would laugh little and weep much, and you would go out to the hills, beseeching Allah for help.» (Bukhari)

If we really understood what is required of us and what lies ahead, we would never even sleep peacefully.

5. Resisting as much as possible the urge to laugh, and trying to stop others from laughing as well. There may be a gathering where people are accustomed to laughing and chatting most of the time. In such scenarios, Muslims must first suppress their own laughter, just as they suppress a yawn; then they should advise others and help them to compose themselves. It takes persuasive, determined and serious individuals to do this. There is a lot of goodness in people, praise be to Allah (ﷻ), and they are ready to respond to the one who wants to reform and improve them. This can be achieved in a number of ways, such as telling them how bad it is to laugh too much and make others laugh excessively because it can lead to lies and falsehood; when a 'comedian' cannot think of a true story to narrate, he fabricates a tale to make others laugh. This is the kind of person who was warned by the Prophet (ﷺ): «Woe to the one who talks and tells lies to make people laugh...woe to him, woe to him!» (an authentic hadith recorded by Abu Dâwood)

It can also make him an unstable person who is held in low esteem by others. This is because the person who makes people laugh is despised by them, even if he thinks otherwise. They have no respect for him at all, and the same applies to the person who laughs too much.

6. Changing the subject that leads to excessive laughter and introducing another, more useful subject. If you see that people

have gone too far with their laughter, try to bring them to their senses using a proper method such as introducing a discussion on a serious topic which will help them make good use of their time. This can also be done by reading a useful book, exchanging ideas, or suggesting some charitable project or other good work that Allah (ﷻ) likes and is pleased with. As a last resort, if you have done all that you can to advise them correctly, get up and leave the gathering to protect yourself from corruption.

﴿... وَلَا تَزِرُ وَازِرَةٌ وِزْرَ أُخْرَىٰ ... ﴿١٦٤﴾﴾ (سورة الأنعام: ١٦٤)

﴿...and no bearer of burdens will bear the burden of another...﴾ *(Qur'an 6: 164)*

## *Waswâs* (insinuating thoughts) from Satan

A person asked: "I am suffering from many insinuating thoughts about the nature of Allah, may He be Glorified. There are thoughts going around in my mind that I cannot utter because they are not befitting to Allah; they keep coming back to me when I am praying and during other times. It is so bad that I doubt my faith and wonder whether or not I am a Muslim. What is the cure for this problem?"

A number of hadiths have been reported from the Prophet (ﷺ) which contain the answer to this problem, praise be to Allah.

The Messenger (ﷺ) said: «The devil may come to any one of you and say: Who created Allah? If any one of you experiences this, let him say: *Âmantu billâhi wa rasoolihi* (I believe in Allah and His Messenger), and that will drive him away.» (recorded by Aḥmad with a good chain of narrators)

The Messenger of Allah (ﷺ) also said: «The devil may come to any one of you and ask: Who created the heaven? and he will say: Allah. The devil will ask: Who created the earth? and he will say: Allah. Then, the devil will inquire: Who created Allah? If any one of you experiences this, let him say: *Âmantu billâhi wa rasoolihi.*» (Bukhari and Muslim recorded similar hadiths)

The Prophet (ﷺ) also said: «Whoever experiences anything of this waswâs, let him say three times: *Âmantu billâhi wa rasoolihi*, and that will drive the devil away.» (a similar hadith was recorded by al-Mundhiri and authenticated by al-Albâni)

The Prophet (ﷺ) said: «The devil may come to any one of you, and say: Who created such-and-such? Who created such-and-such? until he asks: Who created your Lord? If this happens to anyone, let him seek refuge with Allah and let him stop such thoughts.» (Bukhari)

The Prophet (ﷺ) said: «The people will nearly ask too many questions, so that one of them may say: Allah created all of creation, but who created Allah? If they say this, then recite:

﴿قُلْ هُوَ ٱللَّهُ أَحَدٌ ۝١ ٱللَّهُ ٱلصَّمَدُ ۝٢ لَمْ يَلِدْ وَلَمْ يُولَدْ ۝٣ وَلَمْ يَكُن لَّهُۥ كُفُوًا أَحَدٌۢ ۝٤﴾ (سورة الإخلاص: ١-٤)

﴿Say: He is Allah, [who is] One, Allah the Eternal Refuge. He neither begets nor is born; nor is there to Him any equivalent.﴾

*(Qur'an 112: 1-4)*

— and spit [without releasing spittle] to your left three times, and seek refuge with Allah from the devil.» (an authentic hadith recorded by Abu Dâwood)

The Prophet (ﷺ) said: «Think about the signs of Allah; do not think about Allah [Himself].» (recorded in *Ṣaḥeeḥ al-Jâm'i*; al-Albâni graded it as reliable)

The Prophet (ﷺ) also said: «Think about the creation of Allah; do not think about Allah [Himself].» (collected by as-Suyooṭi; al-Albâni graded it as sound)

From these texts, we may summarise the following six ways for people to overcome these insinuating thoughts:

1. People who are experiencing such ideas should recite: *Âmantu billâhi wa rasoolihi* (I believe in Allah and His Messenger).

2. They should seek refuge with Allah (ﷻ) from the accursed Satan by reciting three times: *A'oodhu billâhis-Samee'il-'Aleem min ash-shayṭân ir-rajeem, min ḥamzihi wa nafkhihi wa nafathih.* (I seek refuge with Allah, the All-Hearing, the All-Knowing, from the accursed Satan, and from his slander and evil insinuations.)

3. They should spit (dryly) to their left three times.

4. They should stop thinking about these things, as the Prophet (ﷺ) said: «Let him stop.»

This is an important tactic, because letting the devil influence one in this way will only worsen the situation. Muslims must block these thoughts as much as they can and occupy their minds with something useful and beneficial.

5. They should recite Soorat *al-Ikhlâṣ*, because it describes the attributes of the All-Merciful and is considered to be equivalent to one-third of the Qur'an. Reciting this great soorah will guarantee an end to these insinuating thoughts.

6. They should think about the creation and blessings of Allah (ﷻ) rather than His nature; this is because the weak human mind

can never comprehend His nature. Allah (ﷻ) says:

﴿يَعْلَمُ مَا بَيْنَ أَيْدِيهِمْ وَمَا خَلْفَهُمْ وَلَا يُحِيطُونَ بِهِۦ عِلْمًا ﴿١١٠﴾﴾ (سورة طه: ١١٠)

﴾Allah knows what is [presently] before them and what will be after them, but they do not encompass it [what He knows] in knowledge.﴿ *(Qur'an 20: 110)*

## Staying up late at night

We have received multiple questions about this problem from many people who are searching for a solution. It appears that many people are wasting a lot of time by staying up late at night.

However, the truth is that this phenomenon is not homogenous. There are three kinds of staying up late:

### 1. Staying up late to worship Allah (ﷻ)

This includes staying up for worthy reasons that are of benefit to the Muslims in general, such as engaging in *jihad* (fighting in Allah's cause) and guarding the borders of the Muslim lands, as well as staying up to pray qiyâm al-layl and read the Qur'an. Allah says:

﴿كَانُوا قَلِيلًا مِّنَ ٱلَّيْلِ مَا يَهْجَعُونَ ﴿١٧﴾ وَبِٱلْأَسْحَارِ هُمْ يَسْتَغْفِرُونَ ﴿١٨﴾﴾

(سورة الذاريات: ١٧-١٨)

﴾They used to sleep but little of the night, and in the hours before dawn, they would ask forgiveness.﴿ *(Qur'an 51: 17-18)*

We should not forget, in this context, the noble Companion of the Prophet (ﷺ) who was guarding the Muslims at night and spent his time praying while on guard duty. He was struck by an arrow fired by the polytheists and his blood began to flow, but he kept praying, enjoying his contact with his Lord (ﷻ).

It is reported that some of the scholars used to discuss *Hadith* [the collected statements and actions of Prophet Muhammad (ﷺ) that with the Qur'an form the basis of Islamic law] until the sun came up. Some of the sincere callers to Islam still stay up at night discussing matters about the Ummah which keep them awake. Shaykh 'Abdul-Ḥameed ibn Badees and Shaykh al-Basheer al-Ibrâheemi, founders of the Muslim Scholars' Organization (*Jamee'at al-'Ulamâ' al-Muslimeen*) in Algeria, are an example of this. During their time in Madinah, they used to stay up all night until the time for fajr prayer, discussing the state of the Muslim Ummah and the innovations, myths and backwardness which had become mixed up in it. They would plan how they would rescue the Algerian society from this regretful state.

This kind of staying up is allowed and is entirely worthy, as long as it does not lead to the neglect of something more important or more obligatory. Some people may stay up for a legitimate purpose but miss fajr prayers as a result. This is a serious mistake.

## 2. Staying up for a permissible reason

This is fine as long as it does not lead to the neglect of something obligatory. This includes, for example, travellers staying up to talk to one another in order to relieve the tedium of travel. The Prophet (Blessings and peace be upon him) would stay up to talk to one of his wives and keep her company when they were on a journey, but he never missed the fajr prayer.

This also includes talking to one's guests and keeping them company.

Amongst the permissible reasons is the staying up involved in modern-day shift work to satisfy the demands of worldly circumstances. There is no doubt that the interests of the Muslims demand that some people work at night, such as those who work in the security forces, in hospitals and airports, in supplying electricity, and so on. Again, this should not lead to missing the fajr prayer.

### 3. Staying up to commit sin

This includes watching movies; playing such prohibited games as cards; consuming the flesh of others by gossiping, backbiting and slandering; and other kinds of sins. This kind of staying up is prohibited; those who do it are sinners and deserve the punishment of Allah (ﷻ). Their number has increased in modern times for the reasons mentioned as follows by a poet:

*Youth, idleness and good health,*
*Corrupt man in a bad way!*

It is important to distinguish one type of staying up from the other.

The habit of staying up late at night has become widespread in our times for a number of reasons, including the following:

- Staying up for worldly purposes, as in the case of some traders and business executives who stay up late putting their affairs in order, or students who stay up to study. People in this situation should try to organise their time so that they do not need to stay up late, in order to avoid the negative consequences.

- The nature of modern life and the social changes which it has brought. Earlier generations used to go to sleep with the approach of darkness. The presence of electricity in modern times has led people to become involved in many different activities that were unheard of during the hours of darkness. In some cases, people's nights have become just like their days.
- Widespread indulgence in the modern arts and media by means of television, radio, video, the internet and the like.
- Many people visit their family and friends at night; they organise programs at night as well. This is because of the nature of their work and studies. You rarely come across anyone who will visit you during the day, unless it is the weekend. Even gatherings for the pursuit of Islamic knowledge are held after 'ishâ' prayers.
- Some people indulge excessively in idle chatter and trivial discussions, even disturbing others with their talk and laughter. This phenomenon is perhaps most obvious among students living in university residences, where some inconsiderate visitors stay up late talking about who said what, harming themselves and others and thus neglecting many of their duties.
- Insomnia, which is often caused by indulgence in sin and being far away from Allah (﷾). Being far away from Allah (﷾) means that a person can never feel content or at peace, but will be dogged by constant anxiety and confusion.

Problems with family, money, studies or work also have a clear role in causing anxiety and insomnia. This continues until these problems are resolved.

We should not ignore the fact that some are prevented from enjoying sleep due to insomnia caused by fear of Allah (ﷻ) and a keen desire to reform the Ummah.

Having examined the different types of staying up late and explained the reasons for them, we will now address different ways of treating this widespread problem.

## Treatment from a theoretical point of view

We should think about the physical harm that may be caused by staying up late, along with its many detrimental effects, such as:

- Neglecting Islamic duties, such as missing fajr prayer altogether or in congregation; or praying in congregation without the necessary concentration because of feeling exhausted. In such a state, one fights sleep and fails to understand what is being said. Thus, a person may not even know what the imam is reciting, where he is in the prayer, or what he is saying at the various stages of the prayer. For this reason, the Prophet (ﷺ) forbade conversing after 'ishâ', except on religious matters. (Ibn Mâjah; al-Albâni graded it as sound)
- Physical harm may result from making the night a time for activity and the day for resting; this is contrary to the natural rhythm which Allah (ﷻ) has created in humankind. Allah (ﷻ) says:

﴿وَجَعَلْنَا ٱلَّيْلَ لِبَاسًا ﴿١٠﴾ وَجَعَلْنَا ٱلنَّهَارَ مَعَاشًا ﴿١١﴾﴾ (سورة النبإ: ١٠-١١)

﴾And made the night as clothing, and made the day for livelihood.﴿ *(Qur'an 78: 10-11)*

﴿قُلْ أَرَءَيْتُمْ إِن جَعَلَ ٱللَّهُ عَلَيْكُمُ ٱلنَّهَارَ سَرْمَدًا إِلَىٰ يَوْمِ ٱلْقِيَٰمَةِ مَنْ إِلَٰهٌ غَيْرُ ٱللَّهِ يَأْتِيكُم بِلَيْلٍ تَسْكُنُونَ فِيهِ ۖ أَفَلَا تُبْصِرُونَ ﴿٧٢﴾﴾

(سورة القَصَص : ٧٢)

﴿Say: Have you considered: if Allah should make for you the day continuous until the day of resurrection, what deity other than Allah could bring you a night in which you may rest? Then will you not see?﴾ *(Qur'an 28: 72)*

We can find many people who have gone astray and against their innate nature, suffering from ill health. One hour of sleep at night is worth two at any other time, as is well-known from experience.

❖ Many employees fall short in their work as a result of staying up late. A man may come to work late, in an exhausted state. He might give a poor performance, treating clients badly. If this attitude is habitual, it might even raise the question of whether or not his salary is entirely lawful in Sharia because of the poor quality of his work.

The same applies to students who stay up late and come late to school or university the next day, not caring if they have missed their early classes and barely understanding anything that is said in the classes they do attend.

❖ Staying up late may cause a person to sleep at inappropriate times, such as sleeping after 'aṣr. The early, righteous generations of the Ummah used to dislike sleeping after 'aṣr unless there was a genuine need, in which case there is nothing wrong with doing so. Moreover, sleeping after 'aṣr can cause headaches and make it difficult to get to sleep early at night.

- Staying up late makes it difficult to perform certain voluntary acts of worship, such as devoting the last third of the night to prayer, or getting up to eat the pre-dawn meal prior to observing a voluntary fast. How can those who stay up late manage to do these things? There is no doubt that exhaustion would prevent them from getting up, thus, they deprive themselves of a great deal of good.
- Missing out on the blessings of getting up early in the day: Those who stay up late, end up sleeping until after fajr, thus missing out on the time about which the Prophet (ﷺ) asked Allah: «O Allah, bless the early morning for my Ummah.» (Bukhari)

These people cannot stay in the mosque until sunrise in order to remember Allah (ﷻ), or go out early to earn their living during the time of blessing and virtue. This has become so widespread that you will rarely come across someone who opens his store or business early in the morning.

When wise people realise the various types of harm that result from staying up late, and the great loss that can befall them as a result, no doubt they will try their utmost to reform themselves and make up for what they have missed. Thus, they will take the first step towards solving the problem.

## Practical steps

Listed below are a number of practical steps to be followed by anyone who wants to solve this problem:

1. Trying hard to get used to sleeping early: Staying up late is basically a habit; those who struggle determinedly against their

own selves can win the struggle in a few days, by the grace of Allah (ﷻ), and join the ranks of those who sleep early.

2. Getting married: Many single young men are quite disorganised, staying up late together and encouraging one another to do so because they have no wives or children to think about. However, the one who is married feels his responsibility towards his wife and children; he is keen to return to them early so that they do not worry about him. At times, he feels afraid of being absent in case they need him in the middle of the night. Anyone who has experienced this will understand.

3. Strengthening one's feelings of responsibility in all areas will also be of help: When a man feels the burden of responsibility on his shoulders, he has no choice but to fulfill it. He will not be able to waste time, unlike the careless people who squander the vast treasure of time in trivial matters and do not appreciate the value of time.

4. Adopting the habit of taking an afternoon nap instead of sleeping at the wrong times: Sleeping after 'aṣr or before 'ishâ' is a harmful practice, as we have mentioned above. The Prophet (ﷺ) advised his Ummah to take naps: «Take an afternoon nap, for the devils do not take afternoon naps.» (aṭ-Ṭabarâni; al-Albâni graded it as sound)

These are a few practical measures which one can take to solve the problem of staying up late. Allah (ﷻ) is the One Who guides to the straight path.

# Bad temper

A person complained: "I get angry very quickly. If there is the slightest provocation, I explode and start to break things, swear, curse and issue threats of divorce. This problem has caused me much embarrassment and has made most people hate me, even my wife, children and closest friends. What can I do to rid myself of this awful disease and extinguish this devilish fire?"

Anger is a tendency that comes from the devil. Only Allah (ﷻ) knows how much evil and sin results from it. Hence, Islam has a great deal to say about this negative characteristic; moreover, the Prophet (ﷺ) prescribed multiple remedies for ridding oneself of this problem and limiting its effects. These include the following:

1. Seeking refuge with Allah (ﷻ) from Satan:

«Sulaymân ibn Ṣard said: I was sitting with the Prophet (ﷺ), and there were two men swearing at one another. One of them was red in the face, and the veins of his neck were standing out. The Prophet (ﷺ) said: I know a phrase which, if only he would say it, this [anger] would leave him. If he said: *A'oodhu billâhi min ash-shayṭân* (I seek refuge with Allah from Satan), this [anger] would leave him.» (Bukhari)

He also said: «If a man gets angry and says: *A'oodhu billâh* (I seek refuge with Allah), his anger will cease.» (a sound hadith recorded by Abu Dâwood)

2. Keeping quiet:

The Messenger (ﷺ) said: «If any one of you gets angry, let him remain silent.» (Aḥmad; al-Albâni graded it as sound)

Anger usually makes people lose control, often to the extent that they utter words of disbelief — Allah (ﷻ) forbid — or curses, or words of divorce that destroy their families, or foul language that earns them the enmity of others. Keeping quiet is the way to avoid all of these evils.

3. Keeping still:

«It was reported that Abu Dharr (رضي الله عنه) was watering his animals at a trough when some other people came along. Abu Dharr (رضي الله عنه) asked: Who among you will help me to water my animals? A man said: I will. However, he broke the trough. Abu Dharr (رضي الله عنه) was standing. He sat down, and after a while he lay down. Someone asked him: O Abu Dharr, why did you sit down and then lie down? He said: Because the Messenger of Allah (ﷺ) said: If one of you gets angry, let him sit down if he is standing. If his anger goes away, [that is good,] otherwise let him lie down.» (recorded by Aḥmad; al-Albâni graded it as sound)

According to another report, Abu Dharr (رضي الله عنه) was watering his animals at a trough when another man made him angry, so he sat down...[2]

One of the benefits of this instruction from the Prophet (ﷺ) is that it prevents an angry person from doing something crazy and being out of control. Those who are angry could inflict harm or even kill — as we shall see shortly — or they could destroy property and so on. Sitting down makes it less likely that they will explode in this fashion, and lying down makes it even less likely that they will do something reckless or harmful.

---

[2] al-Mannâwi, *Fayd al-Qadeer*, p. 522.

'Allâmah al-Khaṭṭâbi (may Allah have mercy on him) said in his commentary on Abu Dâwood:

> The one who is standing is ready to move and destroy things. The one who is sitting is less likely to do so, and the one who is lying is not able to do anything of the sort. It seems that the Prophet (ﷺ) commanded an angry person to sit down or lie down in order to prevent him from doing anything that he would later regret. And Allah knows best.[3]

4. Remembering the advice of the Messenger of Allah (ﷺ):

«Abu Hurayrah (رضي الله عنه) reported that a man came to the Prophet (ﷺ) and said: Advise me. He said: Do not become angry. The man repeated his request several times, and each time the response was: Do not become angry.» (Bukhari)

According to another report, the man said: I thought about what the Prophet had said, and I realised that anger is the source of all evil. (Recorded by Aḥmad with a sound chain of narrators)

5. «Do not get angry, and paradise will be yours.»[4]

Remembering what Allah (سبحانه وتعالى) has promised to those who refrain from anger and strive to control themselves is the best way to extinguish the flames of anger. The Prophet (ﷺ) has told us about this great reward: «Whoever suppresses his anger at a time when he could express it openly, Allah will fill his heart with contentment on the day of resurrection.» (aṭ-Ṭabarâni; al-Albâni graded it as sound)

---

[3] *Sunan Abi Dâwood wa M'âlim as-Sunan*

[4] al-Albâni graded it as sound. Ibn Ḥajar attributed it to aṭ-Ṭabarâni. See *al-Fatḥ*.

Another immense reward is described in the hadith: «Whoever suppresses his anger when he is able to vent it, Allah will call him before all the people on the day of resurrection and let him choose whomever he wishes from the most beautiful maidens of paradise.» (recorded by Abu Dâwood and others; al-Albâni graded it as reliable)

6. Knowing the high rank and distinction that is bestowed upon those who control themselves:

The Messenger of Allah (ﷺ) said: «A strong man is not the one who can wrestle another to the ground; a strong man is the one who can control himself when he is angry.» (Aḥmad; the hadith is agreed upon)

The angrier the people get, the more highly valued is their level of self-control.

The Prophet (ﷺ) said: «The man gets intensely angry, so much so that his face reddens and his hair stands on end, but he suppresses his anger. He is a genuinely strong man.» (Aḥmad; al-Albâni graded it as reliable)

The Prophet (ﷺ) used an incident that took place in front of his Companions as an opportunity to reinforce this lesson.

«Anas (رضي الله عنه) reported that the Prophet (ﷺ) passed by some people who were wrestling, and asked: What is this? They told him: So-and-so is a strong man. He beats everyone who challenges him at wrestling. The Prophet (ﷺ) said: Shall I not tell you who is stronger than him? A man who is mistreated by another, but suppresses his anger, has defeated his own devil and the devil of the one who mistreated him.» (al-Bazzâr; Ibn Ḥajar graded it as reliable)

7. Following the guidance of the Prophet (ﷺ) with regard to anger:

He is our role model and example; his attitude towards anger is clearly demonstrated in many hadiths, of which one of the most famous is reported by Anas (رضي الله عنه), who said: «I was walking with the Messenger of Allah (ﷺ), and he was wearing a Najrâni cloak with a stiff collar. He was accosted by a Bedouin who pulled his cloak roughly. I looked at the Prophet's neck and saw the marks left by the collar. The Bedouin said: O Muhammad, give me some of the wealth of Allah that you have! The Prophet (ﷺ) turned to him and smiled, and ordered that he should be given something.» (al-Bazzâr; Ibn Ḥajar graded it as reliable)

Another way in which we may follow the example of the Prophet (ﷺ) is by making our anger for the sake of Allah (سبحانه وتعالى). This means we get angry only when the limits set by Allah (سبحانه وتعالى) are violated. This is a worthier kind of anger. According to several hadiths recorded by Bukhari, the Prophet (ﷺ) became very angry when he was told about the imam who was making people feel bored whilst praying because his recitation was too long. He became angry when he saw a curtain decorated with pictures of animate creatures in 'Â'ishah's house. He also became angry when Usâmah (رضي الله عنه) interceded with him about the Makhdhoomi woman who was guilty of theft.

He said to him: «Are you interceding concerning one of the punishments prescribed by Allah?»

He also became angry when he was asked questions he disliked.

8. Knowing that suppressing anger is one of the signs of piety:

Allah (سبحانه وتعالى) has praised certain people in His book; the Prophet (ﷺ) has highly commended them as well. Prepared for them are gardens as wide as the heavens and the earth. Some of their characteristics have been described in the following verse:

﴿ٱلَّذِينَ يُنفِقُونَ فِى ٱلسَّرَّآءِ وَٱلضَّرَّآءِ وَٱلْكَـٰظِمِينَ ٱلْغَيْظَ وَٱلْعَافِينَ عَنِ ٱلنَّاسِ ۗ وَٱللَّهُ يُحِبُّ ٱلْمُحْسِنِينَ ﴿١٣٤﴾﴾ (سورة آل عِمرَان: ١٣٤)

﴿Who spend [in the cause of Allah] during ease and hardship and who restrain anger and who pardon the people — and Allah loves the doers of good.﴾ *(Qur'an 3: 134)*

These are the people whose good qualities Allah (ﷻ) has mentioned; they are those whom others admire and want to catch up with. Another of their characteristics is that:

﴿... وَإِذَا مَا غَضِبُوا۟ هُمْ يَغْفِرُونَ ﴿٣٧﴾﴾ (سورة الشّورىٰ: ٣٧)

﴿...when they are angry, they forgive.﴾ *(Qur'an 42: 37)*

9. Paying attention when one is reminded:

Anger is something natural; people differ with regard to it. It may be very hard for a person not to get angry. However, if sincere persons become angry and are reminded about Allah (ﷻ), they will remember Him and stay within the limits that He has prescribed. Some examples of this follow.

«Ibn 'Abbâs (رضي الله عنه) reported that a man asked permission to see 'Umar (رضي الله عنه) and permission was given. The man said: O son of al-Khaṭṭâb, by Allah, you are not giving us much, and you are not ruling us fairly! 'Umar (رضي الله عنه) became so angry that he was about to hit the man, but al-Hirr ibn Qays (رضي الله عنه) [who was among the people sitting with 'Umar (رضي الله عنه)] said: O Commander of the Faithful, Allah said to His Prophet:

﴿خُذِ ٱلْعَفْوَ وَأْمُرْ بِٱلْعُرْفِ وَأَعْرِضْ عَنِ ٱلْجَـٰهِلِينَ ﴿١٩٩﴾﴾ (سورة الأعرَاف: ١٩٩)

﴾Take what is given freely, enjoin what is good, and turn away from the ignorant.﴿ *(Qur'an 7: 199)*

— and this man is one of the ignorant.

By Allah, 'Umar (رضي الله عنه) did not take the matter any further after this was recited to him. He adhered to the words of Allah, the Glorified and Exalted.» (Bukhari)

This is how a Muslim should be, not like the evil hypocrite who got angry and was informed about the hadith of the Prophet (ﷺ); he was advised by one of the Companions of the Prophet (ﷺ) to seek refuge with Allah (سبحانه وتعالى) from Satan. Hearing that, he said: Do you think there is something wrong with me? Do you think I am crazy? Go away! (Bukhari)

We seek refuge with Allah (سبحانه وتعالى) from failure.

10. Knowing the negative effects of anger:

The negative effects of anger are many; they harm both the self and others. A person may swear, utter obscenities, and hit others, lashing out without control. It may even lead to killing.

The following story contains a lesson. 'Alqamah ibn Wâ'il reported that his father (رضي الله عنه) told him: «I was sitting with the Messenger of Allah (ﷺ) when a man came along, leading another by a twisted rope. He said: O Messenger of Allah, this man killed my brother. The Messenger of Allah (ﷺ) asked: Did you kill him? He said: Yes, I killed him. He asked: How did you kill him? He said: He and I were hitting trees to make the leaves fall [so we could use them for animal fodder]. He swore at me, so I got angry and hit him on the side of the head with an axe and killed him...» (Muslim)

Even if anger does not go as far as this, there may still be broken bones as well as other injuries. If the person with whom a man is angry runs away, he may turn his anger upon himself, tearing his clothes, slapping his cheeks, falling unconscious, or breaking dishes and furniture.

One of the worst things that result from anger and cause social ills and family breakdown is divorce. Ask many of those who have divorced their wives how and when it happened, and they will tell you: "It was in a moment of anger."

As a result of this 'moment', lives are shattered and children are lost. Feelings of regret and failure haunt people's minds, and life becomes bitter — all because of anger. If only they had remembered Allah (ﷻ) and returned to their senses, restrained their anger and sought refuge with Allah (ﷻ) from Satan, what happened would not have happened. Going against Sharia results only in loss.

The physical harm that results from anger is very serious. Doctors have reported that anger can cause a number of medical conditions such as thrombosis, high blood pressure, fatal heart attacks, diabetes, and so on. We ask Allah (ﷻ) for good health.

11. The angry individuals should think about themselves during times of anger:

If they could see themselves in the mirror while they are angry, they would be able to observe how the colour changes, the face reddens, and the veins of the neck stand out. They shake uncontrollably and behave as if they are crazy. This sight would make them despise themselves. They would be repelled by their own appearance; yet it is well-known that the ugliness that exists inside a person is even worse than that which may appear on the outside. How happy Satan must be when someone is in this state! We seek refuge with Allah (ﷻ) from Satan.

12. Supplication:

This is the constant weapon of the believers. They ask their Lord (ﷻ) to rid them of evils, problems and bad characteristics; they seek refuge with Allah (ﷻ) from falling into the pit of disbelief and wrongdoing caused by anger. This is because one of the three qualities which will save a person from hellfire is being just and fair both during times of contentment and times of anger. (From a hadith recorded by al-Bayhaqi; al-Albâni graded it as reliable)

One of the supplications of the Prophet (ﷺ) was: «*Allâhumma bi 'ilmika al-ghayb wa qudratika 'ala al-khalqi aḥyinee mâ 'alimta al-ḥayâta khayran li, wa tawaffani idha 'alimta al-wafâta khayran li. Allâhumma wa as'aluka khashyataka fil-ghaybi wash-shahâdah, wa as'aluka kalimât al-ikhlâṣi fir-riḍâ wal-ghaḍab, wa as'aluka al-qaṣda fil-faqri wal-ghina, wa as'aluka na'eeman lâ yanfad, wa qurrata 'aynin lâ tanqaṭi', wa as'alukar-riḍâ bil-qaḍâ', wa as'aluka bard al-'aysh ba'd al-mawt, wa as'aluka ladhdhat an-nadhar ilâ wajhika wash-shawqa ilâ liqâ'ik, fi ghayri ḍarrâ' muḍirrah wa lâ fitnatin mudhillâh. Allâhumma zayyinna bi zeenatil-eemân wa'j'alnâ hudâtan muhtadeen.* (O Allah, by Your knowledge of the Unseen and Your power over all creation, keep me alive as long as You know life is good for me, and bring about my death when you know death is good for me. O Allah, I ask You to make me fear You, in secret and in the open; I ask You to make me speak sincerely during times of contentment and during times of anger; I ask You to make me moderate in poverty and in wealth; I ask You for a blessing that does not end, contentment that never ceases, and for acceptance of Your decree. I ask You for a good life after death, and I ask You for the joy of looking upon Your face and the longing to meet You, with no harmful adversity or misleading trial. O Allah, adorn us with the beauty of faith, guide us and let us be a means of guidance for others.)» (recorded by an-Nasâ'i and al-Ḥâkim; al-Albâni graded it as sound)

In light of the solutions provided to these everyday problems, we should try our utmost to incorporate as many of these into our lives as possible. With the help of Allah (سبحانه وتعالى), those who implement the guidelines provided will be able to develop a lifestyle that is closer to the lifestyle of the Prophet (ﷺ). Hence, they will be able to live lives that are far more fulfilled and blessed. Allah (سبحانه وتعالى) knows best.

Praise be to Allah, Lord of the Worlds.

# Glossary of Islamic Terms*

| | | |
|---|---|---|
| *'aṣr* | عصر | mid-afternoon; the obligatory prayer at that time |
| *fajr* | الفجر | dawn; the obligatory prayer at that time |
| *Hadith (ḥadeeth)* | حديث | the collected statements and actions of Prophet Muhammad (ﷺ) that with the Qur'an form the basis of Islamic law |
| *hadith (ḥadeeth)* | حديث | a statement or action of Prophet Muhammad (ﷺ) that was remembered and recorded by his Companions and followers |
| *'ishâ'* | عشاء | evening; the obligatory prayer at that time |
| *jihad (jihâd)* | جهاد | struggle or striving (in Allah's cause) |
| *maghrib* | مغرب | sunset; the obligatory prayer at that time |
| *qiyâm al-layl* | قيام الليل | lit. 'standing the night'; getting up to pray supererogatory prayers during the late night and early morning before fajr; see *tahajjud* |

* The Arabic words are transliterated according to the conventions of the Transliteration Chart found in this book. If a word has become part of the English language (i.e., is found in a dictionary of Standard English), that spelling is used in this book and appears first in this Glossary, with the transliterated form in brackets after it.

| | | |
|---|---|---|
| *Ramadan (Ramaḍân)* | رمضان | the ninth month in the Islamic calendar; the month of obligatory fasting; the month in which the first verses of the Qur'an were revealed |
| *ṣalât or ṣalâh* | صلاة | formal prayer: a combination of physical postures, recitation and supplication |
| *Sharia (shari'ah)* | شرعة | Islamic law derived from the Qur'an and the Sunnah |
| *soorah or soorat* | سورة | chapter of the Qur'an |
| *Sunnah* | سنَة | the practice and collected sayings of Prophet Muhammad (ﷺ) that together with the Qur'an forms the basis of Islamic law |
| *sunnah* | سنَة | acts that are recommended but not mandatory |
| *Ummah* | أمّة | community or nation: *usu.* used to refer to the entire global community of Muslims |
| *witr* | وتر | lit. an odd number: a single unit of supererogatory prayer, to be prayed any time after the evening (*'ishâ'*) prayer and before the call for the dawn prayer |

# Notes

...........................................................................................................................

...........................................................................................................................

...........................................................................................................................

...........................................................................................................................

...........................................................................................................................

...........................................................................................................................

...........................................................................................................................

...........................................................................................................................

...........................................................................................................................

...........................................................................................................................

...........................................................................................................................

# Notes